I'm NOT a BLACK SLAVE DESCENDANT!

I'm **NOT** a BLACK SLAVE DESCENDANT!

AND OTHER WRITINGS

CHARLES RAMIREZ

Library of Congress Control Number: 2021917714

PAPERBACK: 978-1-955955-77-5
EBOOK: 978-1-955955-78-2

Ordering Information:

For orders and inquiries, please contact:
1-888-404-1388
www.goldtouchpress.com
book.orders@goldtouchpress.com

Printed in the United States of America

Contents

Listen To The Crowd Reaction!

Name the time you attended either a live concert or a sporting event and you screamed your lungs out! Your favorite rock star, your favorite Hip-Hop artist, your favorite athlete has come to town and you have front row seats. Describe the feeling you had seeing your favorite performers live…

When you attend any live performance from any performers, describe your reaction. Did you cheer them on? Did you boo them viciously? Or did you do the *worst* thing a fan would do at any live performance – did you sit there in complete silence?

Understand that the worst thing you can do when you attend a live performance is to sit there in *silence*! Whether you know who is performing or whether you don't know who is performing, staying silent is the worst crime committed in attending a live performance. Do not stay silent!

Imagine being the performer. You create new material. You practice and rehearse all this material you've created. Lighting cues, sound checks, wardrobe. Imagine you're a pro athlete. You go to the gym and train. You go to the arena and practice. Imagine being either of those performers you choose to be…

Describe your reaction as a performer when you hear the crowd reactions. Describe your reaction when they cheer wildly for you. *Feel the adrenaline rush!* You have the opportunity to work the crowd's emotional reactions, so what do you do when the crowd starts to boo you? Describe your reaction.

Believe that you have the opportunity to work the crowd's emotional reactions. You can work the crowd *cheering* for you. You can work the crowd *booing* you. That should be part of your training, your practice, and your rehearsals, even though most say it's hard to work their emotional reactions.

Prepare for the *worst*! The last thing you want performing live in front of 20,000+ people is the *silent treatment!* Imagine that…20,000+ people come to see you perform *and all they do is sit there in silence?!* Ask yourself, what can you do to keep them cheering you on?

Watch other performers. Notice how each performer find a way for the crowd to keep cheering them on. If you want to be more creative, notice how some performers find a way for the crowd to start *booing* them! You can even ask yourself what you can do for them to boo you!

Allow yourself to be creative as all possible to work the crowd's emotional reactions! People want to be entertained. You can get them to cheer you, you can get them to boo you, but don't *ever* get them to stay silent when you perform. 20,000+ people and all they want to do is *sit there* in silence during your performances…?!

Sex Objects And Non-Sexual Objects

If most women say they don't want to be treated as sex objects; being whistled to, being catcalled or being approached; *explain these same women enjoying themselves embarrassing and humiliating the non-sexual "Christian" guy for not being sexually attractive.* Explain the double standard they set when they talk to men.

If you're one of those sexually attractive women who say they don't like to be treated as sex objects, yet enjoy yourself embarrassing and humiliating the non-sexual "Christian" guy for not being sexually attractive enough, explain yourself embarrassing and humiliating the non-sexual "Christian" guy. Explain that double standard you set.

Understand that those who give you the catcalls and the whistles and find you sexually attractive are the same ones who enjoy themselves embarrassing and humiliating the non-sexual "Christian" guy wearing glasses…*just like you do!* From that, they like to initiate the gay sexual advances toward the non- sexual "Christian" guy wearing glasses.

Imagine those who give you catcalls and the sexual advances give the non- sexual "Christian" guy wearing glasses. Do you *really* think they're making it easy for that guy too; embarrassing him, humiliating him, even making the gay sexual advances towards him, simply because you're not sexually attractive to that guy, either.

Describe the benefits of being the non-sexual, "Christian" guy wearing glasses. Is he living debt-free? Are his Christian beliefs repeatedly compromised by those who give you catcalls and the whistles? Are his beliefs being used against him just as your beauty is being used against you? Describe the benefits.

They never said they treated the non-sexual "Christian" guy better than they treat you when they see you and they whistle and give you catcalls. In fact, they treat him *worse* – intimidation, assault, blackmail, extortion-you name it. Here you are, getting mad over whistles and catcalls when you walk down the street?!

Most people say this has been going on from the beginning of time. Fortunate few take themselves away from the embarrassment and humiliation and find the right one for them. Then there are those who start trouble wasting time with the women and the guy. *Describe which one are you.*

Describe this writer. Do you think he fits that so-called unattractive, non- sexual guy? Imagine the women he's come across with and not get the sexual attraction from most of them. Imagine the embarrassment and the humiliation he's got in his life. Imagine the silent treatment he gets from most women.

Are you *still* like most women who say you don't want to be treated as a sex object, yet enjoy yourself embarrassing and humiliating the so-called non- sexual unattractive guy and not give him the time of day for not being sexually attractive enough? If not, take the initiative. *Take action!*

Street Credibility...
Or Just Ignorance?

Realize the difference between street credibility and ignorance uplifted. There are those who enjoy themselves keeping you guessing which is which. A *lot* of ignorant things have been passed off as street credibility and we as a people have to take control of this. Too many of the right people are being left out.

Are you from the streets, or do you just *think* you're from the streets and put on a front, like keeping your baseball cap on all day just to look street credible? If you're the latter, you're being ignorance uplifted; *you're not street credibile!*

If there ever was a line that separated street credibility from ignorance uplifted, that line has been blurred and maybe even erased. Some of that ignorance has been taken to the government and the law. There are those who are neither of these qualities that are suffering morally and financially.

Imagine you're talking to someone with street credibility and someone ignorant enough to just go along with the one with street credibility. The one with street credibility has no reason to lie to you. The one ignorant enough to go along with what he says wants to exaggerate. Then what…?

Describe the way you were raised. Did you develop street credibility or were you raised right with street credibility? Were there those who enjoyed themselves dumbing you down and being ignorant with you? Did they keep you from learning? Be aware of yourself. We can't afford to uplift ignorance.

No one was raised the Brady Bunch/Leave It To Beaver households anymore. Those who were are practically invisible. *Phased out!* Most people can't relate to the Bradys or the Cleavers. So what's left? The street credibility and the ignorance uplifted. Everyone has been faced with one or the other.

No matter how long this takes we need to be aware of the difference between street credibility and ignorance uplifted. There are too many descriptions and examples mixed and matched in different people. One can say he has all the street credibility and ends up a fake and vice versa.

There is one who comes to work wearing a baseball cap with braids sticking out looking like he's street credibility but is very ignorant. There is another who comes in looking like he doesn't know but surprises you with his work. Street credibility appears differently with different people. Individuals.

Who can you tolerate more…the one with the street credibility or the one who uplifts his ignorance? Who do you respect more? Who would you respect more? You have a responsibility to yourself to realize the difference between street credibility and ignorance uplifted. Own up to that responsibility now.

Describe The Benefits Blocking Charles Ramirez On Facebook!

Unblock Charles Ramirez from Facebook! What did he do that was so wrong you had to block him on Facebook? How do you know he's what some people who enjoy misunderstanding him says he is? Do you know him *personally?* And how often do you see him on a daily basis?

How often *do* you see Charles on a daily basis? Do you decide to see Charles on a daily basis or is it just random? If you don't decide to see Charles on a daily basis, *how can you judge him by blocking him on Facebook?* Is that fair?!

Understand that you're falling for the all the problems about Facebook. You're not helping the solution, you're *adding to the problem* when you block certain people on Facebook; particularly Charles! Does he really deserve to be treated like this? How can you associate him with the *real* stalkers/hackers?

Suppose Charles was living a decent life. Would you want him to say, *"I'd like to thank you, you, you, and you* (insert names here) *for blocking me on Facebook and having a tough chance to share in my success"?* What did he ever do to you to say that?

Describe the benefits you have *now* blocking Charles on Facebook. Are you working overtime just to stay off Facebook? Are there other people you're seeing who influence you into blocking Charles on Facebook and don't even *know* him?! Do they help you decide not to see Charles everyday?!

Decide who are you going to believe. Do you want to jump to conclusions and follow those who enjoy themselves misunderstanding Charles for you to misunderstand him, blocking him on Facebook? Or are you going to decide to find out what Charles is really like? Make the decision…

Prepare for the consequences blocking certain people on Facebook like you did Charles Ramirez. This writing will probably be the least of your worries. You block Charles and you keep those who enjoy themselves misunderstanding Charles as *Facebook friends*? How well do you know them than you know Charles…?

Notice that you don't see Charles everyday but you do see those who enjoy misunderstanding Charles on a daily basis. Describe the success you need to be wrong about Charles by blocking him on Facebook. Share the opportunities that came with the success blocking Charles on Facebook.

Allow yourself the time to see the wrongs and the mistakes made in blocking Charles on Facebook. Did it really get you *real* success? Are you contributing to the problems of stalkers/hackers on Facebook by blocking Charles, who you rarely see every day? What did he do that was so wrong to you?

Explain the guarantees that came with blocking Charles on Facebook. What did you get out of deciding not to see Charles every day *and* blocking him on Facebook? What did those who misunderstand and don't know Charles give you that Charles himself couldn't? Success? Recognition? Popularity? Opportunity? Hardship? Struggle? Pain? Annoyance?

Facebook has difficulty knowing who are the real people and who are the stalkers/hackers. How can you add on to that difficulty by blocking the *real* Charles Ramirez? If you're convinced that Charles is a good person and you're *still* blocking him on Facebook, what does that say about you…?

Okay, Charles Ramirez isn't perfect. He has his flaws. But who are you to jump to conclusions and decide to block him on Facebook just on misunderstandings? Who are you to just focus on Charles's flaws and build on that by blocking him on Facebook? Are you *that* negative about people in general?

Writing about unblocking Charles may seem like it's been taken too seriously. Then again, describe the benefits blocking Charles Ramirez on Facebook. Ask yourself who's taking it seriously, Charles writing about being blocked on Facebook, or you reaping the benefits of blocking Charles on Facebook. *Who's really benefiting here?*

Unblock Charles Ramirez on Facebook! What is there to gain blocking him on Facebook when you decide not to see him face-to-face on a daily basis anyway? How much hate do you have for Charles to block him on Facebook and not even see him every day to get to know him?

Explain The Definition Of Hard Work

Is it hard work because there is work to be done, or is it hard work because you enjoy yourself bringing hardship to the job? You know who you are, swelling up with pride now that this writer is acknowledging you! Are you *jealous* because people know more than you do?

Hard work doesn't mean hardship! Who are you to enjoy yourself adding on hardships to things that can be done in no time? Who are you to assume some people don't have it hard enough in life? And who are you to enjoy yourself demanding others to do work *you* should be doing?

If you're the one coming to the job thinking of ways to dump more work on others so you can do less work, *explain yourself!* You are NOT above anyone, and you shouldn't bring other people down to your level and make them work *twice* as hard *ten times over.*

At the end of the day, you're strutting along while your co-workers are exhausted wiping the sweat off their heads. *This is equality to you?* This is what's called *Equal Opportunity* to you? How much more important do you have to feel to not sweat it out as much as the others do?

Most people blame corporations for twisting the definition of hard work. Then there are those like *you* who take the definition of hard work and turn it into the *slave mentality.* If you're showing this example more than corporate is showing it, how can you blame the corporations for twisting the definition?

Hard work does NOT mean hardship! Get it through your head now that hard work is NOT hardship! Repetition is the seed of selling: Hard work does not mean hardship. *Hard work does not mean hardship. HARD WORK DOES NOT MEAN HARDSHIP!*

If you can't tell the difference between hard work and hardship, explain the research study showing college graduates looking for jobs outside the United States. Wouldn't *they* know the difference between hard work and hardship? Do you *really* think they're looking overseas just because of the jobs aren't hiring? Imagine that…!

Understand the difference between hard work and hardship. Stop making it one and the same by coming to the job dumping work on others so you can strut around clean at the end of the day. Own up to your fair share of hard work and stop expecting others to have your share of hardship in life.

If you have problems at home, *leave them at home!* How much more important do you have to be taking your problems at home to the job, using company policy as a segue way to release hardship in your life? There IS a difference between hard work and hardship.

The problem is people taking advantage of other people's personal hardships as a motivation, not a problem that needs to be solved. You expect others to have as hard as you do *in life!* So what do you do? You dump more work on others at the job so that at the end of the day they're tired and you're strutting around.

You have a problem not knowing the difference between hard work and hardship! Otherwise *why do you expect others to have it as hard at work as you do in life?* This isn't about company policy, it's about you bringing in hardship to the job and expect it to pass it off as hard work!

Describe any company's reputation. Are they built on hard work or on hardship? If the company is built on hard work then why are you bringing the hardship? Explain why some companies are moving out of the country themselves! Do you *really* think they're moving because it's a better land overseas?

Explain the company's policy on personal hardships. Hard to explain that, isn't it? *Why?* Because *YOU* expect people to have it as hard or as harder than you do, not the company! Companies are built on hard work, not hardship. You enjoy making things harder for everyone else because *you* have it hard!

Maybe you want to talk tough and once again, add on more hardship. Think about this…People will read this and understand and take action should you double up on the hardship. People will see the difference between hard work and hardship and will take action! *HARD WORK IS NOT HARDSHIP!*

Asian-American Culture

Are you looking to learn some Asian culture and customs in this piece? Is there something or someone Asian that you want to know about? Do you *really* want to know all there is about Asian culture? *Read something else!* This is about Asian-*American* Culture! ASIAN-AMERICAN CULTURE IS THE NEW MILLENIUM!

There are generations and generations of Asian-Americans living in America today! Whether they immigrated here or whether they were born here…and there are a *lot* of us who were and are born here…you cannot deny their existence here in the USA. Look next door! Walk into work! There they are…

Describe your relationship with an Asian-American living in your area. Do you just see him or her at work and nowhere else? Are you showing respect to him or her and their background? How well do you know any Asian- Americans living in your area? Do you acknowledge their presence?

Understand where they're coming from. They're not just about their Asian culture. ASIAN-AMERICANS ARE INDIVIDUALS. Build up an understanding that they have learned both Asian AND American culture and were able to create a living from BOTH cultures. Respect how they're living and they'll show you respect back. It's ALL respect.

It doesn't take any time at all to get to know Asian-Americans. The only things that make it difficult for you to understand Asian-Americans are other people's hatred, prejudice, jealousy, and misunderstandings towards understanding Asian-Americans. On the other hand, like you, Asian- Americans want their privacy, too. PRIVACY…NOT INVISIBILITY!

Look around. Go to school. Get ready for work. The proof will show itself. There they are – Asian-Americans living in America. John Cho. The Basco Brothers – Derek, Dante, Darion, and Dion. Tia Carrere. Yellow Rage. Taiyo Na. Anida Yeou Ali. Beau Sia. Giles Li. Bao Phi. And Charles Ramirez.

You acknowledge Italian-Americans, Irish-Americans, Jewish-Americans, Mexican-Americans, and African-Americans. There are Swedish-Americans, German-Americans, and Puerto Ricans, as well as Native Americans. *How is it so hard to acknowledge an Asian-American born and raised here in America?* There are generations and generations of Asian-Americans *born and raised* here. Is it that hard to imagine?

This is an opportunity for you to understand Asian-Americans are *individuals*. Most may know their culture and live that fine line between Asian and Asian-American. Fortunate few are living a success story. Then there are those who were *born and raised* here in the States and learned the American way of living!

Enjoy yourselves recognizing Asian-Americans, whether they immigrated here or whether they were born here. Just because the staff of People Magazine doesn't feature us on the Cover Story on a repetitive basis doesn't mean we're any less American than any of the celebrities featured on the magazine. WE ARE ASIAN AMERICA!

Factions

Describe joining a group that had that inner group you had to measure up to. It's that group of people who were there the longest but formed its own core. Here you are, the newest member, and that inner group executes its own ideas of welcoming you into the group.

Most people had to face this situation more than once in their lives; at school, at work. Fortunate few earned their way through it all. Then there are those whose lives are that much more *boring* they have to manipulate, embarrass and humiliate others to succeed and get comfortable.

Understand those who were in that inner group you had to measure up to then may be the same people now who are enjoying themselves expecting you to work twice as hard ten times over while they don't have to. What if they were having a good time while you work overtime? Suppose they're off spending the money you're supposed to earn?

Imagine the success the people in that inner group are sharing without you. Suppose they're living the success of keeping you out of the spotlight no matter how successful you turned out to be. What if they convinced others to *not be interested* in you and your success? Picture them living the success you deserve and mocking you because you didn't make it.

Describe the life you're living now. Would it measure up to the lives of the people in that inner group are living? Is it measuring up to the lives of the people in that inner group are living *now?* To ask who really cares may explain the reason this so-called competitiveness between you and that inner group is going on!

If most of the people in that inner group are in that position to make your life harder than it has to be, imagine the results. Do you really think these people are flipping burgers at McDonald's or selling Ladies' Shoes at Macy's full- time? Or are they managing the National Debt?

Prepare for yourself, your success, your recognition, and your independence. You don't have to measure up to the success of the people in that inner group just as much as the people in that inner group don't want to *lower themselves* to your high level of living. They're *not interested!* And they respect thewishes of one of their own who's *not interested* in you.

Black Slave Mentality

Are there black co-workers at your job who won't let you forget how hard they have it in life? Do they enjoy themselves intimidating you because you're not a black slave descendant and they know it? Do they seem to cram 400 years of black slavery into an 8-hour work day?

Your skills, abilities, talents, and more importantly, your passion are all being used against you. And it's not just by the company you work for. It's the *black slave mentality.* The one or more persons who come into the job and expects you to work harder than you have to.

This is for you to understand what's going on. Who's watching you work, who's manipulating your abilities for their own benefit, and who's *really* taking your credit for working hard. *You are not a black slave descendant* and you shouldn't be treated like one just because you have a job to do!

Watch what they say. If they're reading this too they're probably coming up with ideas to make the job you work at harder than it already is! They probably don't need to read to come up with hardship ideas when you come to work. It would *explain* this!

Build up confidence in your individuality. Develop an interest in your own family history. If there is no black slave ancestry in your family history, *why are you expected to face, confront, and/or develop the black slave mentality at your job, your career, and your life here and now?*

They never said the black slave mentality isn't the standard of what hard work is today; they just go out and make examples of those who are *not* black slave descendants. They don't have a problem sharing the suffering and the struggle. Listen to their tone and how they go about this.

Some black co-workers are not above making examples out of those who are not black slave descendants. They want to come to work to try to cram 400 years of black slavery into an 8-hour work day…by making an example of the rest of us. Explain their motivation to work…

Go to work today. Clock in and watch your black co-workers. Do they stand back and watch you do all the heavy work and they don't help? That *explains* them expecting you to suffer and struggle like a black slave. Is that *really* company policy? Is that in the Handbook?

Your skills, your abilities, your talents, and your passion should help you build success, opportunities, recognition, security and independence; *not* the black slave mentality. *You are not a black slave descendant!* Your productivity shouldn't be measured by the black slave mentality. *No one* should be measured by the black slave mentality!

Think about the future. Do you want your children raised to believe that the black slave mentality is the standard of hard work when they reach adulthood? That no matter *how* educated they are their work has to measure up to the black slave mentality and not by their own ability?

The problem is this – if the black slave mentality is the standard of what hard work is today, you shouldn't be working, yet here you are. Just because you're not working because you're not a black slave descendant, you shouldn't be homeless and penniless because of it! And you shouldn't face it at your job!

Name one black co-worker at your job who says he's not a black slave descendant and yet expects you to work twice as hard ten times than he does. And at the end of the day you an others are exhausted while the one black co- worker is as fresh as he was coming in earlier that morning.

Describe the people at your job. Describe the people at your job who take pride in skills and abilities in doing their job and producing results on their own abilities. Describe the people who take initiative in doing the job and not be manipulated into doing the job.

Now describe the one person at your job who expects the rest of you to have it twice as hard ten times over simply because you are not a black slave descendant. Describe that one black person who knows you're not a black slave descendant and expects you to build that mentality.

It's that one person instigates other black co-workers into manipulating those who are not black slave descendants into dumping more work onto them. And who would know that better than the Asian-American workers who work so well that one black co-worker makes an example out of them?! ASIAN-AMERICANS ARE NOT BLACK SLAVE DESCENDANTS EITHER! THIS MENTALITY HAS TO STOP NOW!

Describe Yourself Not Liking Charles Ramirez

If you don't like Charles Ramirez, if you don't like Charles writing about the Black Slave Mentality, the silent treatment, the I'm-Not-Interested attitude that comes with the silent treatment, or any other negative element any of you can think of to pin on Charles, stop pinning these on Charles!

Most of you want to take every opportunity to pin every negative element on Charles just to build your ego and look good to the ladies. And most of you ladies take every opportunity to act on these elements too; the silent treatment I'm-Not-Interested attitude towards Charles comes to mind.

This isn't about Charles; this is about YOU: Your words, your silence, your emotions and your actions towards Charles, which are all writing material! He wouldn't be writing about this if most of you wouldn't be like this toward him! Watch your tone and watch your attitude next time you see Charles!

You don't like Charles, why? "It's a standard of living to not like someone just moving into the city"? A popular standard of living.

So you're being a follower that can't think for himself so he has to follow or copy what's popular in a negative way. Grow up out of it!

You got what you wanted when you hurt, embarrassed and humiliated Charles to do the jobs you should be doing. Before Charles came along, you were the one that was hurt, embarrassed and humiliated to do the jobs because of whatever complications you have had at home. Grow up!

Compare yourself not liking Charles to how others are not liking Charles. Compare yourself not liking Charles' writing about the Black Slave Mentality, the silent treatment, the I'm-Not-Interested attitude, to how others are reacting to his writing. Do you really want to be worse than them not liking Charles?

You still don't like Charles. You still don't like Charles writing about the Black Slave Mentality, the silent treatment, the I'm-Not-Interested attitude that comes with the silent treatment, or any other negative element any of you can think of to pin on Charles. Stop pinning these on Charles!

Where are all of you now? How many of you are looking forward to seeing and talking to Charles? How often do most of you want to see Charles again, WITHOUT any negative pre-conceived ideas to hurt, to embarrass, and to humiliate Charles? Where does he fit in your schedule?

How many of you know Charles Ramirez well enough to go around not liking him? If none of you don't know Charles well enough to not like him, and most of you do not know him well enough, how can you say that you don't like him? Keep reading his book! Get to know Charles!

Describe Yourself Watching Charles Ramirez

When you see Charles Ramirez work, when you see him walk, when you see him do anything, tell us your feelings. Do you feel *jealous* of him doing things so easily? Are you waiting for him to make a mistake and pounce on it? Watch how you watch Charles.

Charles doesn't have his own reality show. He doesn't have People Magazine naming him as one of the 50 Most Intriguing People…or one of the Sexiest Men Alive, for that matter! Is that why you don't watch Charles? Or is that why you do watch Charles for other reasons?

Do you feel a sense of *failure* on yourself when you watch Charles do right? Is there a sense of satisfaction if you see Charles make a mistake? Do you feel better about yourself watching Charles? Ladies, do you enjoy watching Charles Ramirez? How do you ladies feel watching him?

You think nothing of it when Charles does something for you, don't you? Most of you took *so much* advantage of watching Charles do something for you, you get selfish thinking you're getting ahead of Charles in life. Do you want to watch Charles come and take it all back?

Most people watch Charles do right. Then there are those people who enjoy watching Charles *suffer, struggle,* and be *humiliated.* Which one are you? Are you watching Charles *at all?* Do you ignore watching Charles because he's not the standard-bearer? The measuring stick of success? The image of life for you?

If at any time you see Charles, watch him carefully. He is the epitome of the Asian-American. People Magazine didn't name him the Sexiest Man Alive, so why should Charles get more than his fair share of that rejection from non- subscribers like you watching him so non-sexually, ladies?

Maybe Charles doesn't do that much when you watch him; that's because Charles Ramirez *is not a slave descendant.* And what Charles does gets results done. Those who enjoy themselves watching Charles struggle may be slave descendants *themselves.* Do you enjoy watching Charles struggle because he's not a slave descendant?

Imagine an Asian-American born in South Philadelphia (Naval Hospital), Raised in Willingboro, NJ and now living back in Philadelphia starting a new life. *That's Charles Ramirez!* Watch him live his life the way he wants to. Build up an interest for Charles Ramirez. Imagine the benefits watching Charles living life!

Look around you. How many Asian-Americans have you watched who didn't kill themselves fighting in martial arts films? How many Asian-Americans have you just walked by without giving a second glance? How many Asian- American reality shows are there? Watching Charles Ramirez is a learning experience. Watch Charles do his thing!

You'll develop a sense of open-mindedness when you watch Charles. He's not and overachieving Asian, but he's not a hustler either. Charles has been exposed to many good and different things in life that you can watch him without discrimination. That's what you should do…watch Charles without discrimination!

Few people enjoy themselves watching Charles Ramirez in a very discriminate way. Those are the people who you should avoid. They may not know Charles *personally*, so they'll enjoy themselves telling you lies about Charles. So if you have a question to ask Charles, ask him *directly.* He has nothing to lie about himself.

Charles has people who watch out for him, and Charles watches out for them too. If you enjoy watching Charles, do so in a very respectable way. Those who enjoy watching Charles be embarrassed and humiliated do so in a disrespectful way. Don't do what they do. Watch Charles respectfully. Watch him do right.

Those who enjoy themselves watching Charles be embarrassed and humiliated are not watching out for Charles *but for themselves.* They may say they're watching out for Charles but it's for their *own* selfish reasons. They don't want to watch Charles succeed over them. They want to keep him down. That's wrong.

Imagine watching Charles Ramirez doing good. In fact, don't imagine, just watch Charles do good and in time, Charles Ramirez will do something great! So, stay tuned and don't touch that remote, as they say. Watch Charles Ramirez each and every day here in Philadelphia! Enjoy watching Charles Ramirez do right!

If I Forgive You...Then What?

Are you looking for forgiveness from Charles Ramirez? Are you *demanding* forgiveness from Charles to a point of *intimidation* and *reckless endangerment*? If you didn't forgive Charles easily, explain yourself expecting *him* to forgive *you* so easily. You're the one wanting Charles to be humiliated and embarrassed almost to death!

If you don't forgive Charles so easily, explain yourself expecting him to forgive you so easily. You're *such* the standard; the measuring stick of forgiveness, right? Not Charles, so you think. If Charles forgives you, then what? You embarrass him. You humiliate him. You expect him to do good.

Understand the trust issues you have in Charles. You lost so much trust in Charles, yet Charles still has trust in you. Describe the ambivalence you feel when Charles enters the room. That ambivalence shows the loss of trust you have for Charles. Do you want Charles to lose trust in you?

Imagine the life you made in not forgiving Charles. Describe the people in your life who you think are way better than Charles that you forgive them so easily than you do him. Imagine the success you have from not forgiving Charles. You can't? Maybe it's because *you're living it!*

Describe yourself not forgiving Charles. Describe the silent treatment ambivalence you show Charles for not forgiving him. Describe the embarrassment and the humiliation you want to put Charles through just because you don't want to forgive him so easily. Describe the irresponsibility you have for not forgiving Charles so easily.

People say they're big enough to forgive, but they're smart enough never to trust you again. Describe the success in that. Explain the benefits from losing so much trust in Charles. Describe the people who lost so much trust in *you* that you turn around and lose trust in Charles.

Describe the last time you saw Charles Ramirez. Do you even *remember* the last time you saw him? Was it the time you lost trust in him that you can't bring yourself to forgive him? If it was, how can you say you didn't build a success not forgiving him?

Describe the physical role that Charles has in your life right now. Do you invite him to your house for dinner or some other occasion? Or do you expect the worse in him that you don't ever want to see him again? Describe the initiative you take to trust Charles again so he doesn't feel this about you anymore.

If you want nothing to do with Charles…this explains all the writing. Do you enjoy the exposure? You're *already* enjoying the success, now comes the recognition! Is this what you want…letting people know you haven't forgiven Charles Ramirez? How small do you want to live in this world?

You have difficulty forgiving Charles. You have difficulty trusting Charles. You have *so* much difficulty accepting Charles so much you want to push him away from you straight to the wrong element.

Then you wonder why Charles, as good a person as he makes himself, is how he is today.

Enjoying your life now? This isn't to say that Charles didn't forgive you...if it takes you so much time to forgive him, what makes you think he has the time to forgive you? He *can* forgive you; you just made so much an example of him on taking your time forgiving him.

Asian-American Couples

Is there an Asian-American couple in this country who are as successful and as popular as Jay-Z and Beyonce? Or Prince William and Kate Middleton? Do you know of *any* Asian-American couple who are as big as the two couples mentioned? Where is the equality in this if you choose not to know?

There's always been a well-known African-American couple. There's always been a well-known white American couple. But when there's an Asian- *American* couple, the question is always the same: *Who are they?* It's time that there's a well-known Asian-American couple *everyone* can recognize as much as Jay-Z and Beyonce and Prince William and Kate Middleton.

How often do you have to either go online, pick up a magazine or watch, Jay- Z and Beyonce either about their private life, their appearances, or their performances? How often do you have to either listen about Prince William and Kate Middleton's tours, who they're speaking to and what they're wearing?

There are generations and generations of Asian-American couples who are doing just as much work as Jay-Z and Beyonce and Prince William and Kate Middleton do. People Magazine and

US Weekly just don't send out their writers and photographers to get the story or take pictures of Asian-American couples here.

How much longer do Asian-American couples have to live invisibly? Why shouldn't their names be well-known instead of made-up just so some people can enjoy themselves embarrassing them? The time to recognize Asian- American couples by their individuality is *long* overdue! Asian-American Power Couples, *reveal yourselves to America!* Where are you?!

Look around your neighborhood. You can't say there's not *one city* in this country that has an Asian-American couple living a success as big as Jay-Z and Beyonce or Prince William and Kate Middleton are. Once again, People Magazine and US Weekly don't send out their writers and photographers to get the story and take pictures of Asian-American couples.

You have an open mind, don't you? If you're up for equality, why shouldn't there be a well-known Asian-American couple America can know and love and recognize? Why shouldn't there be a well-known Asian-American couple who are up there with Jay-Z and Beyonce and Prince William and Kate Middleton? Imagine…

You will know better than what the media wants you to know about Asian- American couples, whether they're Chinese-American, Filipino-American, Vietnamese-American, Cambodian-American, or Korean-American. And there are more Asian-American couples and individuals here in America. Lao-American, Japanese-American…so many of them to list here…they are a *huge* part of America today.

So when you hear about an Asian-American couple living a success in America, enjoy learning about them. There are those like the media who would rather not let you know about them other than the lies they make up about Asian-American couples or Asian-America in general. Enjoy.

Senior Yearbook Photography Editor 1990

Your senior high school yearbook photography editor. The last person who makes you either one of the most memorable students in high school or one of the forgotten students. Other than your class picture, your club group picture or your graduation picture, what other pictures of you were in the yearbook?

Whether you were caught in the moment many times or just have your graduation picture, the senior yearbook photography editor has that option to make you the most popular or the forgotten. Which one did *your* senior yearbook photography editor make you? One of the most popular or the forgotten?

Understand that option the senior yearbook photography editor has. When you attended your high school reunion, how many of the students do you remember? How many students forgotten attended the reunion? Did most of the most memorable students attend the reunion or most of the forgotten show up? Think back…

Imagine the life the senior high school yearbook photography editor is living now. If you were one of the most memorable students, is your life measuring up to what the photography editor made you? If you were one of the forgotten, is your life exceeding more than what the editor expected?

Describe your life now compared to what the senior high school yearbook photography editor made you then. Are you measuring up to what the photography editor made you, or are you working twice as hard ten times over because the photography editor forgot about you so much you weren't pictured as much in the yearbook?

Allow yourself some time to think about your senior high school yearbook photography editor and the life the editor is living now. What do you want to say to your senior high school yearbook photography editor now? Was the senior high school yearbook photography editor one of the most memorable or the forgotten?

If you're in high school now or even a senior in high school, know who will be the yearbook photography editor. Remember, this will be the last person who makes you one of the most memorable or one of the forgotten students at your high school. Enjoy your high school life!

Be careful what the senior high school photography editor will caption on your photograph! The photography editor will just show your class picture, your club group picture or your graduation picture and nothing more, making you one of the forgotten students. No one wants to be embarrassed one final time.

Ask yourself, do you want to be remembered in high school, or do you want to be forgotten in high school? It's up to you. The senior high school yearbook photography editor may just as well be...*not interested*...in taking pictures of you, just like *this* writer's high school yearbook photography editor.

Facebook People

Of the seven hundred million Facebook users (and counting), how many of them were ever featured in People Magazine? How many of them were ever pictured in the Star Tracks section of People Magazine? Chances are, most of the seven hundred million never *were* the featured story on People Magazine.

If you were featured repeatedly in People Magazine, would you be on Facebook? Would you even have a Facebook page? Do you really think any celebrity featured in People Magazine have the time to log on to Facebook? All the featured stories on People Magazine, would you be on Facebook?

You're not on Facebook because everyone else is, are you? You're on Facebook because there won't be a chance in hell People Magazine would do a feature story or even a *cover story* on you! Do you see yourself pictured in the Star Tracks section? It's not about passive-aggressive disorder.

Imagine the things you post on Facebook; the like and comments you get from posting statuses and/or pictures…or do you get a lot of likes and comments on your Facebook statuses and pics? Now imagine the feature/cover stories and pictures People Magazine would publish about you.

Describe your life if you were featured in People Magazine compared to the life you have now having a Facebook page. Describe the attention you'd get from being featured on People Magazine compared to the attention you get on Facebook. Describe the differences being featured in People and being on Facebook.

No one said you will never be featured in People Magazine, just like no one said you will never be this "Facebook Stalker". This is the one thing People Magazine and Facebook have in common… you'll have your fair share of haters. But if you're not featured in People, how is it a fair share?

Describe the statuses and pictures you post on Facebook that can be the subject of a feature story or pictured in the Star Tracks section People Magazine can publish about you. Describe the moments you post on Facebook feeling like what you have to post can be published in People Magazine.

Notice the numbers. Seven hundred million plus Facebook users. Seven hundred million plus people whose stories won't be published in People Magazine. Why else would seven hundred million plus people become Facebook users? Don't you want to be featured in People Magazine at least once if not repeatedly or vice versa?

If you have some event going on in your life that you post on Facebook, wouldn't that event be good enough to be featured in People Magazine? Don't you think you can be the cover story on People Magazine? Imagine yourself pictured in the Star Tracks section in People Magazine.

Enjoy posting statuses and pictures on your Facebook page! Show the writers and photographers of People Magazine what they're missing out on not doing a feature story on you or publishing your picture on their Star Tracks section of their magazine. Regardless of the guarantee you are good enough to be featured in People Magazine!

Celebrity. Popularity. Recognition. Fame. Fashion. And of course, Money. All those qualities People Magazine is noted for. Yet there are seven hundred million Facebook users like yourself. How is that *not* popularity? How is that *not* recognition? How id that *not* fame, fashion, and money? *How is that not all of that?*

Describe the popularity and recognition you get on Facebook compared to the popularity and recognition you would get if you were the feature story or pictured in the Star Tracks section of People Magazine. Describe the repetition you'd get from being recognized and popular on Facebook than you would in People Magazine.

Describe your Facebook friends. Describe your Facebook family. The comments you make and the comments you get from your posts and your pictures. Describe the likes you like and the like you get from your posts and pictures. Describe the fan pages promoted and the fan pages you like.

Now imagine the friends you make if you were the feature story or repeatedly pictured in the Star Tracks section of People Magazine. Imagine the individuals you'd meet after being featured and pictured in People Magazine. Imagine the connections you'd make if you were in People Magazine. Think about it…

Just because you have a Facebook page and you have a lot of Facebook friends who you know and *don't* know very well does not mean you don't deserve to be featured and pictured in People Magazine! Keep that option open. People Magazine *does* have its own Facebook page, too!

Describe Yourself Embarrassing And Humiliating Charles Ramirez

Are you interested in Charles Ramirez? Do you keep in touch with him? If you were to see Charles after so many years, describe your feelings. Is the success you made in life keeping you from thinking about Charles, how he's doing and what he's doing? If so, you're *still* living in that success *embarrassing* him!

Think about it…are you still living in the success you've made embarrassing and humiliating Charles? You want to maintain that standard of success and make sure Charles doesn't match up and live up to your life, don't you? This is how you want nothing to do with him!

Is this success *really* for you? Is God telling you to live the success knowing that you've embarrassed and humiliated Charles Ramirez beyond His Word? Are you using God and His Word as an *excuse* to maintain this success? Ask yourself these questions when you're all by yourself.

Share the benefits the success got you. Don't just think about the money, because Charles isn't looking for a handout, *unless you have $1000.00 to give to him!* Share the value. Share the recognition you got from embarrassing and humiliating Charles. Share the people you've met and surround yourself with.

Most people would probably want to follow up on your success and embarrass and humiliate Charles. Why? Because *you're living a success at it!* You want nothing to do with Charles and you're living a success at it! And you wonder why Charles is *writing* about you? THIS IS THE MATERIAL YOU GAVE HIM ABOUT YOU!

Notice how long you've lived this success of embarrassing and humiliating Charles. Oh, yeah, you're living a *Christian* life! God has *blessed* you with this success! If at any time you see Charles Ramirez again, are you going to enjoy yourself rubbing that success in his face? Oh, *that's* a Christian thing to do!

Charles Ramirez struggled to maintain his mother's home so she can have somewhere to live her golden years. He *suffered* the embarrassment and humiliation from friends of yours because you succeeded in doing those things. He was homeless for a year. How much more important does your success mean *now?*

Look at your life now. Do you have a family from the success you made embarrassing and humiliating Charles? Are you living debt-free because of the success you made embarrassing and humiliating Charles? Re-evaluate your lifestyle now. Ask yourself, *Did I achieve all the success just because I want nothing to do with Charles?*

Who is to say your success embarrassing and humiliating Charles will last? Who is to say you didn't succeed in embarrassing and humiliating Charles? Who said your success embarrassing and humiliating Charles didn't bring you *more* success? No one said there's a guarantee for success but you proved them wrong at Charles's expense, didn't you?

Describe the difficulties that came along in maintaining that success you made embarrassing and humiliating Charles Ramirez. Foreclosure? Death of a loved one (mother)? Credit debt? Homelessness? Natural disasters? These are what the difficulties Charles *himself* faces for *your* success! Lost his mother's house, lost his mother, paying credit bills, etc.

With the success you made embarrassing and humiliating Charles, those difficulties were easy to overcome for you, wasn't it? You don't have those difficulties Charles had, did you? You're *so much more successful* than he is. You're in that higher standard of lifestyle Charles isn't and you don't want to share it with him, do you?

Describe the people you share your success with; the success you made embarrassing and humiliating Charles. Do they share your belief, or do you have them fighting your battles? Are you going to have them surround you when or if you see Charles again? What would you do…?

You can say your success in life isn't built on embarrassing and humiliating Charles Ramirez; however, if you don't care about Charles and you don't want to keep in touch with him, wouldn't you be living the success *anyway*? If you're *not interested* in him, aren't you living that success?

Imagine building a success *with* Charles Ramirez instead of at his expense.

You've already lived that up, didn't you? You've lived up and are *still* living a success embarrassing and humiliating him. Now imagine building a success with him. If you can't, you're making this piece worth more than he wrote it.

Best-Selling Artist

Are you a fan of Asian-American music artists? When you talk about Asian- American music artist, do other people ask questions like, *Are they from here? Do they live in America? Who are they?* Do you ever as why your favorite Asian-American music artist isn't as recognized as Rhianna, Taylor Swift, and Drake?

Rhianna, Taylor Swift, Drake, and other artists are known to be best-selling music artists. But when Asian-American music artists become best-selling artists, most people in America ask themselves, *Who?* This writer can't even mention one because of this disparity! There are so many young Asian- American music artists deserving to be Best-Selling Music Artists!

Listen to their music. Attend any of their performances. You may even meet them face-to-face easier than you can with Rhianna, Taylor Swift, or Drake for security reasons. See for yourself whether these Asian-American music artists deserve the Best-Selling title. Open your mind. Listen to the music. Listen to the lyrics.

If Taylor Swift traded her western guitar for the ukulele, would she still be a best-selling artist? If Drake traded his rhymes for Taiko drums, would he still be a best-selling artist? If an Asian-American music artist performs pop, rock, R&B or Hip-Hop music, *why shouldn't he or she be a Best-Selling artist?*

There are those in the music industry who persuade you into thinking specific artists are the best-selling artists in the world. You as a listener and a music lover have a choice of who's a best-selling artist. An Asian-American music artist can't be the Best-Selling Artist?! *Are they serious?!*

Name *any* Asian-American music artists who should be the Best-Selling Music Artist recognized as much as (if not *more than*) Rhianna, Taylor Swift, Drake, or any rock, Hip-Hop, R&B, and pop artist today. Listen to their music. Listen to the lyrics. *Let the industry know.*

There are those in the music industry who take advantage of those artists who say, *I only love making music.* When an Asian-American music artist makes that statement, those in the music industry jump to conclusions assuming the Asian-American music artist doesn't want to be the Best-Selling. THIS HAS GOT TO STOP!

How many times do you have to hear about an artist talk about the struggle, the suffering, and the hardships he/she had in the past, and then he/she becomes the Best-Selling Music Artist because of those qualities *rather than the music itself?* Does the music industry expect the listeners like you to suffer more?

Are you expected to relate to the struggle, the suffering and the hardship to enjoy a recording artist's music and make him or her the Best-Selling Artist? Ask yourself, *What is the artist promoting, the music or the suffering the artist faced in his or her life?* How much longer does the hardship to be repeated in music?

Imagine being a music artist. You make the music. You write the lyrics. You practice and rehearse all hours of the day. You release your CD and music to the public. You do all the work to be the Best-Selling Music Artist…*and all the people talk about are Rhianna, Chris Brown, Taylor Swift, and Drake.* How would you feel?

Now imagine being an Asian-American music artist. You work at all the things mentioned above. You self-promote, tour, and release your CD to the public *just as any other music artist.* Yet it's the other artists who get featured *repeatedly* in magazines, the internet and on television. *Why* not *you?!*

People in the music industry say they can only feature so many artists. So why are the same artists featured *all the time?* How much longer does an Asian-American artist's work be so invisible and unheard in America? Yes, there's YouTube and other outlets but some people are being deaf and blind.

When you listen to an Asian-American artist's music, enjoy it! You never know that Asian-American artist may be the Best-Selling Music Artist you have never heard of…and *that's* what some in the music industry are co- depending on you to feel…never hearing about a Best-Selling Asian- American Music Artist. LET THE ASIAN-AMERICAN BE THE BEST- SELLING MUSIC ARTIST OF ALL TIME!

Drifted Apart...Or Just Didn't Want To Be A Friend Anymore?

Do you remember who your friends are? When was the last time you spent some *real* quality time with your friends besides chatting on Facebook, texting or Skyping? When a friend or friends drift apart from you, do you try to re-connect or do you let it be?

This writer isn't the only one who had friends drift apart from him. He isn't the only one who tried to re-connect with old friends and they look at him like they don't know who he is anymore, making him feel like he doesn't measure up to their standards anymore.

What about *your* friends? Do you keep in touch with the friends you made in your life, or have they drifted apart from you? In this day and age people measure the kind of friend you are by how much embarrassment you can take rather than the friendship itself.

Do you trust your friends enough for them to drift apart from you and come back years later, feeling the both of you can pick up where you left off? Or was it so long ago neither one of you remember where to pick up where you two left off?

Take as much time as you can to re-connect with old friends. Even though the both of you made new friends along the way, is it the same? And where does it say you can't make your circle of friends bigger? Losing friends can be heart-breaking. Take it from this writer.

This writer knows a lot of people who he considers friends. Most of his friends may feel the same way he does. Fortunate few of his friends are his *real* friends. Then there are those who take advantage of him *saying* he's friends with him. Some even *chose* to drift apart.

Own up to re-connecting with old friends, even if some friends choose not to re-connect, offer the opportunity. Who knows? Drifting apart from old friends shouldn't mean the end of the world, so how come some of these friends are so quick to drift apart from you? Is that fair?

Describe the one moment when you and your friends mutually agreed that you all should be friends. If there are even more than one moment you and your friends kept the bond then there's that guarantee you have friends for life. Drifting apart shouldn't even be an issue for you, guys!

Trust. Encouragement. Security. Extended family, as some might say. These are the benefits of having friends you can count on. Of course, there's respect and honor too. Do you really want to go through life feeling that the friends you made in your life *all* drifted apart from you?

How many friends have you lost over a heated argument or a fight? How many friends have you lost over the smallest detail? How many friends have you lost because of work, moving away, or going away for college? How many friends took the initiative to re-connect with you *without* social media?

Fights. Misunderstandings. Drama. Manipulation. Jealousy and envy. How can these make a friendship *stronger*? Why do these negative qualities take so much credit in making a friendship stronger? There are those who take so much pride in being bad they take so much credit in making a friendship stronger. Who really needs those guys?

Enjoy re-connecting with your old friends. *If you love somebody set them free. If they come back it was meant to be.* Remember that? Don't let the drifting apart come in the way of the moments you shared together as friends. Even if it's hard to do, just stick around for them.

Black Entertainment

Most people grew up on Doo-Wop, Jazz, R&B, and Motown. Fortunate few grew up on Hip-Hop – Grandmaster Flash, KRS-ONE, Eric B & Rakim, MC Lyte, Run-DMC. Then there are those now growing up to the sounds of Nicki Minaj, Drake, and others who got most of us asking, *What is this?*

Black Entertainment lost a lot of its souls and conscienceness. But don't blame the artists. Don't blame the industry. Blame it on those who influence the artists and the industry; those who we, as viewers and listeners, don't see contributing to the art and music. The people in the industry listen to those on the street. If some of those on the street aren't right, why are we quick to blame the industry?

Where do *you* fit in? Did you grow up to Motown, Jazz, R&B and Doo-Wop? Were you into Hip-Hop when it was at its finest in the eighties? Or are you listening to the music that's out there now? Describe the era you feel black entertainment was best.

You don't expect black entertainment acts to be perfect, but can you *really* relate to a Hip-Hop or R&B artist whose criminal record is bigger than his best –selling music record? Imagine the artists out there making music who *doesn't* have criminal records.

This is your opportunity to bring back the soul and conscienceness in black entertainment. Why does black entertainment always have to be so close to the struggle, the suffering and the hardships rather than the ease, the healing and the simplicity? How much hardships do you have to feel to enjoy black entertainment?

Describe the artists and industry insiders who did come from the streets compared to the artists and industry insiders who educated themselves and built up their artistic crafts. Who had the final say on what and who the fans, the people, like and want to hear and see? Ask yourselves…

You grew up on Motown. You grew up on R&B. You grew up on Hip-Hop. You didn't grow up on the struggle, hardship, suffering and difficulty. Those were expected of you to face. How much longer do you have to be reminded of the struggle and the hardship every time you listen to a Hip-Hop or R&B artist, or see them in magazines, websites, and on TV?

If you don't voice your opinion on the standard of black entertainment, if you allow the fading out of the soul and the conscienceness of black entertainment, there will be no guarantee of where it will go in the next five or ten years. Then the pain and suffering will endure.

Good music. Lyrics. Stage presence. Performances. Image. These are what's in it for you in black entertainment. You can create good music. You can add lyrical content. You can set the stage and lights. You can choreograph the show. Then maybe the soul and conscienceness will reveal themselves to all.

Black entertainment has lost all its soul and conscienceness to record companies' policies and practices. So many people want a piece of the success of black entertainment they come up with the *craziest* ideas for the artists to look so outrageous fans look at them in a different way. And then…

Berry Gordy was on Tavis Smiley's show several years ago. He said the one misunderstanding people had in him is that he was *gangster.* He stated he wasn't gangster. He was successful. If you want to distinguish yourself from other record companies, be a success.

The cost of black entertainment has gotten so high it took the soul and the consciencenesss. If you're and artist entering the industry *do not lose yourself!* Most people are asking themselves, *What does all this worth?* They get blinded then they start to see again.

To Help You Or To Own You?

Are there people who demand things from you just because they "helped" you to where you are today? Do they take advantage of you? Do you see the truth in their motives even though no one else does? Do they got you doing embarrassing things and enjoy themselves *owning* you?

There are people out there taking advantage of those in need. These people take help one step too far and "take ownership" on you. They think you owe them *more* than you think. Remember the phrase, *give them an inch, they take a mile*? Ask yourself, are they helping or are they owning?

You don't need to be owned like this. You don't need the embarrassment, the humiliation, the suffering and the struggling. You don't need to be taken advantage of. You know what you can do. You don't need anyone enjoying themselves using you for their gain. You are your own person!

People take one look at you and come up with embarrassing and humiliating ideas about you just to enjoy themselves. They come up with ideas of how you should work, the key word her being *should,* then when you make that one tiniest mistake, they make a BIG production out of it making it look like you can't be trusted.

You're not their property! The time for your independence from this is now! They can't own you and come up with humiliating ideas for you to do. You have no time to have your success built on someone taking advantage of what you can do. Take the time to revolt!

Look at how they approach you. Watch how they pull you away from public view and tell you what they want from you. Look at how they come from behind you every time they need something from you. Listen how they like to counter with whatever you say or talk about how things get done.

You can help yourself. Take the initiative to get things done. You're the only one who knows what you need in your life. Don't let anyone come along and take advantage of you. You have a responsibility to yourself to help only you. Ask yourself, *Are they helping me, or are they owning me?*

When you help yourself to the things you need in life, you can look back some day feeling proud of yourself. You'll reminisce on how everything came to be. What you do will attract the right people into your life. And when you help yourself in a positive way, things will take place.

Look at what life has to offer to you when you help yourself. This isn't about being greedy or egotistical even though those are the qualities associated with helping yourself. This is about who is out to get what you got. Only you know what's in it for you when you help yourself.

Annoyance. Larceny. Robbery. Theft. Extortion. Fraud. Blackmail. These are the problems to avoid when asking for help. These are the examples of the phrase, *Give them an inch, they take a mile.* Embarrassment. Humiliation. Suffering. Struggle. These are the results of being a victim of those crimes. So always help yourself.

You may have faced one or more of these problems at one time or another in your life. You have helped yourself out of these problems. You have had people help you out of those problems. People relate to your problems and help you out. *HELP you, and not OWN you!*

Enjoy helping yourself in your life. Watch for the thieves, con artists, robbers, blackmailers, and extortionists hiding in plain sight who at first will *say* they'll help you, extend their hand, then won't let you go on your own will. They're only helping themselves *for themselves.* You help yourself before helping others. Enjoy helping yourself!

Unjust Deportation

Your family. Even though you don't see them as often as you do, if an outside organization comes along and takes away *any* member of your family, what do you do? The breadwinner of your family is taken away, and then what? Suddenly, you're struggling harder to make ends meet.

There are organizations targeting family members and deporting them out of the USA. Organizations coming together invading one family after another. These organizations are *funded* by your tax dollars! Their main goal is to break your family apart against your wishes! Immigration and Customs Enforcement heads these organizations deporting families!

Look at your family. Yes, they get on your last nerves and there are moments when you don't want to see them again. Do you want Immigration and Customs Enforcement come to your home and make that decision for you? *Absolutely not!* What makes you think other families do?

Why should you trust what Immigration and Customs Enforcement say about themselves unjustly deporting family members from their homes? Are they going to give you all the facts or are they manipulating your own securities? What really makes you think that after they deport *all* immigrants, Immigration and Customs Enforcement won't go after *your* family?

Think about it…what if Immigration and Customs Enforcement were able to deport every single immigrant in the USA? What do you think they'd do next? *Who* do you think they'd go for next? Do you *really* think they won't change their policies after deporting all immigrants in this country?

Check their website ice.gov. if you can't find what you need, that's saying something about Immigration and Customs Enforcement. There are websites that are helpful to you to prepare yourself in the event Immigration and Customs Enforcement comes for *your* family. Onelovemovement.com can link you to any and all websites against unjust deportation.

This is about your *family.* Your mother. Your father. Your son. Your daughter. Your brother. Your sister. Your cousin. Your niece. Your nephew. Your uncle. your aunt. This is about *all* your family staying together. No branches broken! Your responsibility is to your family! Immigration and Customs Enforcement shouldn't be taking it from you!

Your guarantee *is* your family! Who knows your family better than you do? Immigration and Customs? They just want you to *believe* they do. They co- depend on you to feel irritated towards your family members. They co- depend on you living without them. They co-depend on you living too independent from them.

You and your family can face Immigration and Customs Enforcement through planning, preparation, knowledge, understanding, and more importantly, love and unity. Keep your family together and in the know. That's what's in it for you. It's what's for your family. Work with your family and keep it in your family.

Breaking up families is what Immigration and Customs Enforcement does. They're being no better than those who break up your family through rape, murder, assault, battery, and even reckless endangerment. Unjust deportation is no different from them! They're deporting good people while ignoring the criminal offenders who hadn't reformed and are "building businesses".

How much more do you owe the government for them to fund an organization like Immigration and Customs Enforcement? How much more in debt do you and your family have to be? Immigration and Customs are funded by your tax dollars! And all they want to do is *deport people and break up families!*

Enjoy your family. Enjoy the times you have with your family. Enjoy the get- togethers and enjoy the long distance communication; the texting, the Skyping, Facebook, Twitter. Enjoy the food, the movies and the shows you share with your family. Enjoy the fight with your family. Enjoy your fight with your family against unjust deportation.

No Snitching = No Recognition

Are you a victim of a crime? Is your criminal offender hiding in plain sight and he's making you feel that you can't do *anything* about it? That you can't snitch? If you snitch on your criminal offender, wouldn't you be giving him what he always wanted… *popularity and recognition?*

If it's your criminal offender's business to rob, harass, humiliate, and attack you, why can't you publicize it like any other newspaper? *Snitch!* Tell the world! Describe all events! Explain the situation! Share your feelings! Walk us through the details! *He's* building his criminal business through *you*! Go snitch!

If your criminal offender is building his business on you, your skills, your talents, and your abilities, where's your percentage? Scars? Cuts? Bruises? Where's your moral percentage? You can't keep quiet *all* the time. Your offender is co-depending on you to explode and make you look bad. It's his business…

Trust yourself. You know what's right for you. Say your offender's name. Say what he's done to you. Say his criminal acts against you. Make him the criminal celebrity Don Corleone, Tony Montana, and Nino Brown are. Go on tmz.com and report your situation. Or just go to your local police station and report it.

So long as your criminal offender is harassing you, it won't take long for society to recognize him. If you think about it, you're probably not his *only* victim. Do you think you're his first? Do you really think you're his first victim? His previous victims may be around you.

Look at the popularity and recognition he's getting at your expense now. And he says you can't snitch on him? You can't make him popular for his criminal acts against you? He wants to be recognized but wants to keep it on the down low?! *Announce him to the world!*

Your criminal offender is owning up to you on his criminal acts, his success on them, and your humiliation. Own up to the responsibility on yourself! *Snitch!* Let the people know about his criminal acts. Some of the people might know already and need a voice! YOU BE THE VOICE!

The first thing you criminal offender would do is go along with what you say about him. If he starts lying, tell the people to look at how he's manipulating them and you. Remember all the humiliation he gave you because he's expecting you to forget. He'll guarantee you will…

Your criminal offender co-depends on you by making you look like you co- depend on him just to live. He says things like, *I'm letting you breathe, aren't I?* Snitch on him and you'll regain control of your life and independence. It's all about you and him. It's not like he's not getting more ideas to humiliate you.

Your criminal offender is expecting you to suffer, struggle, and stress out more than you have to in life. Snitch right and you'll be relieving yourself of these unnecessary problems your criminal offender is enjoying himself putting you through. Your embarrassment is his enjoyment. Snitch about him enjoying himself harassing you.

This all wouldn't be written down if this problem is always with all of us. Prepare yourself. Tell the people. Your friends. Your family. File reports. File restraining orders and other documents. Relieve yourself of the suffering, the struggle and the stress your criminal offender enjoys putting on you.

Are you the only one he's harassing? What if you're not the only one? Imagine the other people he's offended. Organize. Ask around. Advertise. Set up a website. Go online. *Snitch! Snitch! Snitch!* Make your criminal offender more popular by organizing his other victims. His "fan club", so to speak.

All it takes is *preparation.* Organize your family and prepare them for other criminal offenders who say it's open season for them to target your family. Since it is well-known that if a person snitches his family is targeted why hasn't that family organize against this yet? All you have to do is *prepare yourself.*

If you don't even know you criminal offender's name, snitch anyway! Chances are, he'll probably have criminal aliases too. Make an announcement if anyone knows who your criminal offender is; if anyone has been a victim of your criminal offender, too; if anyone live near your criminal offender and doesn't even know it.

There's no such thing a bad publicity, right? So *snitch!* Your criminal offender will love the attention, the popularity, and recognition he's getting from you, even if you don't mention his name. People will feel you. Popularity and recognition are what your criminal offender is co-depending on you to give to him.

Enjoy snitching on your criminal offenders. Make it a publicity stunt. They *love* the popularity and recognition, *don't they?* Well… *snitch!!* Make them popular! Get people to recognize your criminal offender! Watch where his criminal success will take him. Set him up for something or someone tougher than you. Enjoy snitching!

What To Wear? What To Pay?

You step out of the house wearing clothing so *fashionable,* so *stylish,* you're struggling to keep the roof over your head, to keep the lights on, and to keep your stomach full. You step out of the house expecting others to struggle more, if not as much as you do, and look it.

Are you living beyond your means so much you can't even get a decent meal for your own family? Does your appearance mean that much more important than your stability? Your home? Your conscience? And now you step out of the house wearing your pants halfway on your ass?! *Really though?*

Look at yourself for a minute. If you're not dressing yourself so far up, you're dressing yourself so far down. No matter which way you dress yourself, your mentality still stays the same. Even if you dress yourself up so fashionably, your mentality and your vibes dress you down.

Those who admire your appearance, those whose appearance clash with yours, those who come from where you do, or even say they come from where you come from…do you really think they care how you look? You can step out looking like a million bucks and still struggle…like them.

You take so much time on dressing yourself up that you have no time for anything else. Describe the number of times you rushed to do everything else just so you waste time dressing yourself. Yeah, you developed a decent sense of time management for yourself, didn't you? *Did you even shower?*

Look at yourself again for another minute. Aren't you the proof? Do you really think your spending habits on shopping for clothes *doesn't* make it difficult for you in the long run? An empty fridge? No water running? No lights in the house? Is your appearance really worth all of these?

You'll have bigger responsibilities in your life. You got to keep your house. Keep your kids in school. You'll grow up and you'll see for yourself how shallow your fashion sense is compared to other responsibilities you'll be having to take on. So grow up out of this fashion sense.

There will be those who will co-depend on you for other things. Those who will depend on you to do things they need you to do. Your appearance will mean nothing to them as much as your skills and your ability to work with them will. Family, friends, associates, *anyone.*

Security. Independence. Value. Aren't those important to you? Do you really think your fashion sense isn't going to get you robbed, assaulted, or even killed? Is this a real definition of independence to you? This is really defining your worth? One more time…*look at yourself for a minute!*

Enjoy stepping out of the house wearing clothing so *fashionable* and so *stylish* while you still can. There will be those who will enjoy themselves thinking of ways to embarrass and humiliate you or even neglect you and act like you're not there even if you get hurt, because it's all about you, right?

I Shouldn't Listen To Them?
They Shouldn't Be The Only Ones
Talking To Me!

Those of you ladies who chose *not to be interested* in talking to Charles Ramirez, describe the moment that led you to choose not to take the initiative in talking to Charles anymore. Explain yourselves *not being interested* in talking to Charles. Share the success you made *not being interested.*

Liars and manipulators (guys) took advantage of you not taking the initiative in talking to Charles. He doesn't know what they told you ladies about him to make you choose not to be interested in talking to him. Did you *ever* build up an interest in talking to Charles? Why not?

Stand out from the rest of the ladies who chose *not to be interested* in talking to Charles. He doesn't have People Magazine naming him one of the Sexiest Men Alive. Why? Not because there are ladies not interested in talking to him, but they're living a success at not talking.

Charles Ramirez is a good person who has had the wrong people in his ear interested in talking to him. He doesn't need to be judged on that. Understand that and you'll see Charles in a different way. Charles will be your friend, your confidante, and ladies, maybe even your *lover.*

Prepare yourself for anyone who comes to you talking like they know Charles Ramirez. This explains why you should *always* go to the source. If Charles didn't say anything about himself to you, what makes you think those who enjoy themselves lying to you about Charles is the truth?

Listen to the silence. Look at how the ladies barely notice Charles until the liars and manipulators (guys) enjoy themselves embarrassing and humiliating Charles with jokes, insults, put-downs and attacks. Notice the opportunity some ladies *give* these liars and manipulators to embarrass Charles, and wonder why Charles always keeps to himself when he's around others.

Describe the success you need to have in life *not being interested* in talking to Charles Ramirez, ladies. Walk us through the times you ladies had it so easy in life not to be interested in talking to Charles. Imagine what would happen when you take the initiative and start a conversation with Charles *first.*

You will be the lucky lady that successfully got Charles Ramirez out of that *not interested* image some ladies chose to see him as. You will have Charles' gratitude. You will be able to prove the world wrong about Charles. Charles Ramirez will be faithful to you!

There's a difference between not knowing Charles Ramirez and not *wanting* to know Charles Ramirez. If you don't know him, you don't know him. If you don't *want* to know him, you're allowing the fear to build your success in life, as some of those ladies who chose *not to be interested* in talking to him.

Liars and manipulators are interested in talking to you ladies, saying how good you look, how sexy you are, complementing you. Most of them may have even gone so far as complementing you so good they broke your heart at the end! Imagine what they said about Charles Ramirez. Just imagine.

Do you enjoy yourself embarrassing and humiliating guys with jokes, insults, put-downs and verbal attacks? Is that the only kind of talk you do? Is this why *you're not interested* in talking to Charles Ramirez; because you talk just like those liars and manipulators? Describe the success talking like that…

If Charles Ramirez shouldn't listen to the jokes, insults, put-downs and attacks, those liars and manipulators shouldn't be the only ones *interested* in talking to Charles, don't you think, ladies? Take the initiative and start a conversation with Charles Ramirez before the liars and manipulators do.

Sleeping Around

Describe your thoughts on sleeping around. Have you ever thought of sleeping around with members of the opposite sex? Are there certain precautions that come to mind? How often do you sleep around? Do you ever find the time for the right person to sleep around with? Nightly or on weekends?

If you're a lady who's looking for a gentleman to sleep with, there's someone who will find the time to sleep with you. No, he doesn't have the reputation of sleeping with a lot of women! He just has the time to sleep with you, if you will make time.

Understand that this is all about *timing*. Most people need their 8+ hours of sleep. Fortunate few find the ones they sleep with regularly. Then there are those who find the time to sleep around with members of the opposite sex. Who will you find the time to sleep with?

Imagine the person you would like to make time to sleep with. Imagine the person you would like to make time to sleep around with. Ladies, imagine the gentleman you would like to sleep around with. Look around and see who you'd like to sleep with!

Describe what you like in bed. Do you like rose petals, scented candles, and soft music? Are you one of those who just like to jump right in and *get it started*? Ladies, would you like to sleep with this gentleman on a nightly basis? Describe your feelings sleeping around.

There are so many people who will be quick to talk bad about sleeping around. Knowing the person you're sleeping with well enough to sleep with, their health history, or even if they even have a reputation of sleeping around with so many members of the opposite sex. Then again…

Get ready to enjoy yourself sleeping around. Most people are working 40+ hours a week for so long that they don't even find the time to even *sleep,* let alone sleeping around! It's not just a moral thing anymore. Sleep is a *necessity!* Make time to sleep and sleep around!

Notice you're working yourself almost to death! You have people expecting you to work 40+ hours a week. They're cramming 400 years of slavery into an 8-hour work day. Hustle is the only word being used. Jobs are depriving you of sleep. Describe the last time you had 8 hours of sleep.

Allow yourself to sleep around! Find that someone and ask them if they'd like to sleep around with you. You can be exclusive or you can ask for no strings attached. We're living in an era where sleep is becoming unnecessary anymore. *We have to make time to sleep around!*

Enjoy sleeping around! Sleeping is good for the body, mind, and the soul. The body needs the rest. The mind needs to sort things out. And the soul needs to be nourished. What better way for those 3 elements to get what they need than 8 hours of sleep?

Understand Where You Come From, Or Suffer And Struggle The Same Way Now?

Understanding where you come from, where you lived and what you been through and you expecting most of us to suffer and struggle the same way are *two different things*! How do you know most of us aren't suffering and/or struggling now just because we don't show any of it?

If you're expecting most of us to suffer and struggle through life the way you did here and now, you're not making us understand where you come from. You're dumping your problems on most of us and we don't have the time for that! *Don't confuse the two!*

Understand that if you don't want to repeat the suffering and the struggling you went through in your life, you shouldn't try to pass it along with anybody else! Each person has his or her own personal battles, so why do you expect most of us to suffer and struggle more?

Suppose some of us don't want to be reminded of the suffering and the struggling you came from? Suppose most of us have uplifted ourselves and got out of the suffering and struggling by the Graces of God Himself? What benefits you bringing back the suffering and struggling to those who uplifted themselves?

Describe the expectations you have on most of us to suffer and to struggle what you went through and what you're going through now. If most of us have our own personal battles, why do you enjoy yourself adding on to the suffering and struggling? That's not solving anything!

Believe that everyone has their own personal struggling and suffering. If you do believe that, why do you insist on adding on to the suffering and the struggling everyone is going through personally? Who in their right mind would lie about suffering and struggling in life? Are you that *blind*?

Take the time to understand. Just because you're from the streets doesn't mean most of us have to suffer and struggle the same way. Suffering is suffering and struggling is struggling, *whether you're from the streets or not!* All of us are suffering and struggling! Do you really think we have it easy?

Notice the world around you. School closings. Unemployment. Unjust deportation. Pay disparity between management and employee. Rape. Murder. Domestic violence. No one is having it easy! To think there are those who are benefiting from all of this because most of us do not face most of these sufferings and struggles.

Don't expect most of us to take the suffering and struggling you seem to enjoy yourself dumping on us! How much more important do you have to be to dump problems on some of us? How much more self-respect do you need to expect most of us to suffer and struggle in life?

"Our" Government

Do you always wonder who *else* is running the government other than the President and Vice-President? Do you know who the Secretary-Of-State, Speaker Of The House, or any of the Senate members are? Imagine being the President tolerating these government officials' contradicting ideas that oppose the President's. just imagine that…

Who are you quick to blame in the government for what America is going through economically, politically, and morally? You can study Political Science thoroughly and successfully and face contradicting ideas opposing the ideas you have for the government. You have that opportunity to make the government *better*!

Everyone is feeling the same thing you are – the government is corrupted or in bad shape. If you have the skills, the knowledge and the heart to work in the government, *show it*! Show the people and show those government officials who you are and what you're made of.

You have to get them to trust what you say! If you have ideas that can solve most if not all of this country's problems and the so-called bureaucracy within the government, stand by your ideas and get the people by your side. Take time to study those already in office.

Whatever you do, make time for your ideas for this country. If you have the opportunity to talk to the President and/or the Vice-President about your ideas for the government and America… *make the most of it*! Introduce yourself, present your ideas, let them get to know you. Take it!

Look at the condition this country is in now. Political corruption. Debt. High prices. Poverty. Tax breaks for the rich. And who looks rich today? Criminal organizations. Drug dealers. The Middle Class is practically *non-existent*, and there are those who are working in the government keeping it that way!

Aren't you living in this country? How often did you vote each election year? Did you feel your vote counted? Do you feel that your vote counts now more than ever? If you have the opportunity to work in this prestigious government corrupted by debt and poverty, *own up to the solutions!*

You have the opportunity to talk to the President as often as anyone else in this country! How often is the President out of the White House? If there is some sort of restriction on you not to contact the President when you're a government official *yourself,* challenge that restriction!

The opportunity to work in the government can be the most honorable, most prestigious, most important positions anyone who has the chance to enter. If you get the opportunity to work in the government *take it!* You get to learn what goes on inside the government more than anybody else!

The government is the only organization to maintain, protect, and run this country called America. But do you *really* know who is running the government? You know who the President,

Vice –President, Governor, and Mayor are. Who else do you know? Who is really in the President's ear as often as possible?

Enjoy the opportunity to work in the government. Solve the corruption, the debt, the poverty and the greed. That is what the government is built to do. Some people say it's supposed to do that, but they don't have the opportunity to go in and actually work it out!

Accusing Someone As A Stalker

You sexually flirt with one or more guys, but when one flirts back with you you're quick to show fear. You lose all your trust in him and fear builds up in you. Why? Maybe it's because the one who flirted with you didn't "fit" the emotional standard you imagined yourself.

You build success and independence on the fear you feel for the one who flirted with you. It's in the back of your mind as you work to achieve what you need in life. You convince the authorities. They get quick to your fear and label the guy dangerous when all he needs is intimate love.

Ask yourself, *do you really need to build success, independence, and recognition on the fear you have on the one who needs your love?* Is all this really for you when you know it's at the expense of the one who flirted with you before? What is it all worth?

How well do you know those who are accusing him as a stalker than you know the man himself? All the good qualities this accused stalker has before…all of a sudden they're no longer in existence? Did you really lost that much trust on the guy that you can't rebuild the good into the great?

Do you really want to waste time judging this person as a stalker? How much time does it really take to rebuild trust in one person? You say that person doesn't take the initiative…*you're* not taking *any* initiative facing the fear. You're building success on fear!

How much is this person worth in your life? Do you even care? *Are you interested?* You can pray to God that he's doing well all you want to, but if your success in life is built on the fear you have on the person because he has feelings for you…isn't that contradicting your prayers for him?

Own up to the fear! Face that fear and build trust and confidence in that person. The world doesn't need you to make any more stalkers! Why build your life, your independence, and your success on making the authorities quickly make someone you know a stalker? Life is too short for this.

Describe the guarantee you have living the fear you feel that builds your success and your life. The guarantee you have living the fear you have in your stalker that you have to *completely* ignore him. Describe it all. Suppose he dies before you get the chance to see his redemption.

You have the opportunity to eliminate the *fear,* not the person. You have chances to take the initiative to build up the confidence to see the good this accused stalker had in him before the accusation. What does the fear have for you to succeed in life? When was the last time you've seen him?

If you build up the respect and the confidence to no longer see your stalker as your stalker, you will be the one responsible to eliminate this staler epidemic fear the world currently lives in. this is what the world live in now…the fear of being stalked. But everyone shouldn't be accusing this one guy.

Suppose the problem isn't in the accused stalker everyone's accusing, but the fear you feel in yourself. Suppose it's the fear that's the problem everyone is feeling for you. Once again, how much does this fear has to build your success and your life? It's not the accused stalker, it's the *fear!*

Enjoy loving your life now that you've read this. This isn't to liberate all the stalkers out there, just those who don't deserve to be called a stalker because he doesn't "fit" the emotional standard of the Sexiest Man Alive. This isn't for the *real* crazy ones who stalk you.

Explain The Interest Hollywood Had On Jackie Chan

Name any Jackie Chan movie. As a matter of fact, name one outtake in any Jackie Chan movie where Jackie did not injure himself or where he did not nearly *kill* himself performing those martial arts stunts. Name any movie where Jackie Chan did not injure or nearly kill himself!

If you can't name any movie Jackie Chan made where he didn't injure himself or nearly kill himself, you're not the only one. Hollywood wanted Jackie Chan at a time when Hollywood showcased younger male actors with sexual attraction. Ben Affleck. Matt Damon. Leonard Di Caprio. Tom Cruise. Even Denzel Washington!

Understand this question: *Was Hollywood only interested in Jackie Chan's martial arts talent, or was Hollywood only interested in Jackie Chan injuring himself and nearly killing himself just to make other male Hollywood actors that much more sexually attractive to the female audience?* Name any other Asian-American actor Hollywood wanted.

Imagine you're an actor proficient in martial arts. Hollywood is interested in making a movie with you. You injure yourself making the movie and keep going until the movie is finished. Hollywood releases the movie and think it's funny releasing outtakes of you injuring yourself. *How would that make you feel?*

Describe *your* interest in Jackie Chan. Did you like him for his martial arts, his comedy, or did you enjoy yourself watching the outtakes of him injuring himself and nearly killing himself? Ladies, were you sexually attracted to Jackie Chan injuring and nearly killing himself? What did you like from him?

Hollywood never said anything about Jackie Chan injuring himself and nearly killing himself making these movies. They never objected to it, especially when it comes to making other male actors look good to the female audience that much more. They never wanted any other Asian-American actor with sex appeal.

Here it is, years later, and Hollywood *still* isn't interested in making Asian-American actors as big a star as Jackie Chan. Maybe it's because they expect younger Asian-American actors to measure up to Jackie Chan's proficiency in the martial arts…or nearly kill themselves just like Jackie did?

Look at Jackie Chan now. He wants to be taken seriously as an actor! He feels he's not measuring up to Robert DeNiro's or Al Pacino's level of acting. With all the movies he's made, Jackie Chan feels he's not measuring up to Robert DeNiro and Al Pacino?! *Figure that!*

Name any Asian-American male actor now that deserves Hollywood recognition, whether he knows martial arts or not. Name any Asian-American actor now who can break that expectation Hollywood has of what Jackie Chan brought to Hollywood. Not *all* Asian-American actors are like Jackie Chan. Think of any Asian-American actor out there.

Do you want Hollywood to keep on featuring Asian-American male actors as these expendable martial artists who injure themselves, making them unattractive to the female audience, or do you want Asian-American male actors recognized as leading men featured in any genre of movies and breaks the mold?

Of all the talented Asian-American male actors in Hollywood then and now, Holly wood was only interested in *Jackie Chan*? Explain the interest Hollywood had in Jackie Chan. Was it for his martial arts talent? Or was it for his expendability, injuring and nearly killing himself for entertainment purposes? *Which was it?*

If you don't like how Hollywood featured Jackie Chan and if you don't like how Hollywood *still* doesn't feature younger Asian-American male talent, do something about it! Make that change! Name any Asian-American male actor you can think of that can break everything! Everything meaning stereotypes, disparity, invisibility, and prejudice.

Committing Suicide

Are you one of those people who believe that those who commit suicide are weak? Do you swell up with pride, thinking that the person who took his or her own life, didn't measure up to your selfish standards? Did someone you know commit suicide because he or she didn't measure up to you?

This isn't about religious beliefs anymore. Most people have their *own* beliefs about suicide, and the most common belief is *the person is weak.* How much hardship has to be doubled up in a person's life to end in suicide? There's usually more than one person contributing to a suicide.

Are you one of those people who expects others to measure up to you so much you enjoy yourself making everything hard for that person? Do you double up on the hardship towards the person when they're feeling hurt? Do you expect the person to go through the same hardships you do?

People say you don't go to Heaven if you commit suicide. You like to take that one step further and expect so much from someone you have to make life so hard he or she had to contemplate suicide. You enjoy yourself manipulating someone to commit suicide. You trust so much about people not going to Heaven if he or she commits suicide.

You say life is too short to commit suicide. It's not worth one's life. Right, it's not worth one's life to commit suicide. The question is, *Is your life worth someone else's for him or her to commit suicide because he or she didn't measure up to you?* Who's next to commit suicide for you?

This writer had to face more than one person expecting him to measure up. This writer was *repeatedly* embarrassed and humiliated so much that he contemplated suicide. Those who embarrassed and humiliated him are living a success off this. This writer can even *name* them!

Those who embarrassed this writer is probably reading this and reveling in their success. Are you one of them? Do you want to own up to success this way? Yeah, the person took his or her own life just for *you* to gain success in your life. Is that what you want to own up to?

There will be people who will look at you and just *know* you're the reason someone committed suicide. They'd see how you'd act when you work, how you treat others, how silent you are, and the success you gained from someone else's suicide. No one will let you forget this.

What's been in it for you expecting so much from someone you had to enjoy yourself dumping hardship after hardship after hardship on a person to a point of suicide? How many suicide deaths must build up your success in life? How much comedy material do you need in life?

You expect people to have it as hard as you have it in life. You expect people to be embarrassed and humiliated as you were in life. You expect people to relate to you when you don't want to relate to them in return unless you expect them to have it hard in life.

When someone commits suicide from all the hardship you expect them to take in life, you're quick to call them *weak!* You're quick to judge them! You're quick to lie about how you've been treating them all this time! It's *your* selfishness and expectations that can contribute to someone's suicide!

Who are the people who taught you to expect so much hardship from someone to a point of suicide? Family? Friends? Co-workers? Former co- workers? How much do you owe these people to go out and expect so much hardship from someone to a point of suicide? Are you getting paid for this?

Hardship is not the solution to suicide. Harsh judgment is not the solution to suicide. Expectations are not the solution to suicide. When someone you know contemplates suicide, don't think they're not feeling you thinking they're weak. Your share of hardships in life won't help their situation. Show some *understanding.*

Old School Faithfulness

Do you ever wonder why married couples get divorced so suddenly? Is there quite a few more single people living in your neighborhood? Are there elderly couples you see holding hands and are still living together? Are you living single, happily married, or bitterly divorced? You need *Old School Faithfulness!*

Old School Faithfulness is a feeling. It's a feeling that's very rare these days. You hear people hooking up, you hear people holding back, you hear people breaking up. Old School Faithfulness is a feeling when you look at a lady and feel there's no other but her! *No other!*

Ladies, are you looking for a man who you feel there's no other but him? Do you look at your grandparents and wonder how did they stay together for as long as they do? Doesn't anyone, male and female, want that someone special to spend life with? *Feel the Old School Faithfulness!*

Most people don't know what Old School Faithfulness is because most people don't feel the faithfulness! This may even be a new concept to most people because they just heard of the term! There may even be some married couples who don't know what Old School Faithfulness is. They don't!

Stand by your lady not because you have to, but because you're *faithful* to her! Stand by your man not because you have to, but because you're *faithful* to him! Don't feel like you have to, feel the faithfulness to be with the person through thick and through thin.

This writer's parents were in a car crash in 1980. The father died. The mother only had a fractured arm. She lived on for another 23 years before passing away in 2003. She was not interested in seeing anyone but the father again. *That,* dear readers, is Old School Faithfulness!

Build some faithfulness to the one you feel there's no other. Be honest with yourself when building up Old School Faithfulness. Devote some time with that special someone. Take care of that Faithfulness by taking care of the one like no other. Strengthen the Faithfulness and share it with your loved one.

Faithfulness will come back to you tenfold when you share that same Faithfulness with the one who's like no other. Faithfulness will take you farther than money, fortune or fame can *ever* take you. It will all be about the Faithfulness! Prove to yourself that the Faithfulness is within you!

Faithfulness is what's in it for you. You can welcome it and eliminate any form of greed, envy and anger from your life. What would you want more? Power, money, all the materialistic things in the world? What would success be without someone to share it with? It's Faithfulness!

Prepare for the worst when you look for the one that is like no other. There is a chance most won't be feeling this Old School Faithfulness. Then there are those who are liars. Some may be with someone else and won't tell you until it's too late. Prepare yourself.

When you do find the one who is like no other, the both of you enjoy the Old School Faithfulness! It may be brand new to some but keep that Faithfulness. It is a feeling rarely felt today. Keep the Old School Faithfulness feeling. Do not let anyone corrupt the feeling!

Equality

Are you a female who constantly has to prove herself in this "man's world"? Do you feel you can do more than what's expected of you because you're a woman? Is there more opportunity for a woman like you to succeed and be independent than any other time in history?

Girl power and equality has been going on for centuries. Now here you are, 2014 going on 2015, work has been done, yet more work has to be done. You're gaining more equality, ladies. There are so many of you living successfully and independently! Keep on doing what you're doing.

It's all for you, ladies. Opportunity. Success. Development. Independence. Security. Value. Preparation. Investments. You got your knowledge to get you all of those things and more. It's one opportunity after another. Planning and preparation. All you got to do is *do.* Before you know it, things will fall in place.

Trust in yourself. Hope for the best. Prepare for the worst. You know there will be those who will enjoy themselves making things difficultly annoying for you, just because you're a woman. You have that genuine intuition when someone is telling you the truth or when someone is lying to you.

If you plan right, prepare for what's the most conflicting occurences, seize that opportunity and protect yourself, this will be over in no time at all! Plan, prepare, seize, and protect. Any other idea you can think of do not hesitate to include! This is about you, your life, your independence, and your success.

Prove to yourself! You are the only one who has to prove to yourself. Every day you have to look at yourself in the mirror. It's not just for putting on makeup, is it? This is about equality. You're not alone. There are so many women facing this. You're not alone.

Own up to your success. Own up to your abilities that can take you to places you have ever dreaming of. This isn't about passing something on down to you. It's about you taking the opportunity of what to do with what you can do. You can own it all!

Make your own guarantee. No one else can make this guarantee for you. If you can plan, prepare, seize, and protect for yourself, the guarantee can present itself...if you can see that too! There will be those who will plan to take it all away from you.

Whatever is in it for you will present itself too. It's all there for you to take and enjoy. Whatever's in it for you is yours. Don't cheat yourself out of anything! People shouldn't be telling you what's in it for you if they're out for themselves...

They Think Charles Is Thinking...

There are those who think they know what Charles Ramirez knows just because Charles is a nice guy. There are those who are so *jealous* of Charles they *think* they know what Charles is thinking and instigates trouble for Charles with other people. They enjoy themselves instigating trouble for Charles with other people.

When these people approach you and start enjoying themselves instigating trouble for Charles with you, let it be known that they *think* he said what he said or he did what he did. If didn't hear it *directly* from Charles Ramirez *himself,* who is one of the most honest people around, it's a lie!

Understand these people may be the same people you enjoyed themselves instigating trouble for *you* with others! Do you really think they haven't told Charles lies and rumors about you? Don't give them time to enjoy themselves instigating trouble for you or for Charles! It only takes a minute...

Imagine these people enjoying themselves instigating trouble for you on a repetitive basis, just because life is so *boring* for them. Imagine these people have nothing better to do with their lives other than instigating trouble with *everybody.* Imagine these people instigating trouble to a point of committing a crime.

Describe the time these people enjoyed themselves instigating trouble for you with somebody else. Now these people want to get the chance to enjoy themselves instigating trouble for you with Charles Ramirez! Do you really have the time for this instigation these people enjoy themselves with? Neither does Charles!

They said Charles said it, they think Charles is thinking it! If you did not hear it from Charles Ramirez himself, nine times out of ten what they said Charles *may* have said is a lie! What they think Charles is thinking is a lie! Charles never said it, Charles never thought of it.

These people will take every chance they get enjoying themselves instigating trouble with you and Charles. Their lives are so dull and boring they want our lives to be just as dull and boring as theirs. They're gonna say you said something and nine times out of ten it would be a lie.

The person with the baseball cap on with braids sticking out enjoys himself instigating trouble for others by speaking so softly he enjoys himself lying to you, he dumps work on you just to instigate more trouble for you. He thinks you're thinking you know and instigates trouble for you.

Describe the person in your life similar to the one mentioned above who enjoys himself instigating trouble for you. Describe the number of times he enjoys himself holding it over your head that he instigated trouble for you and got away with it. Describe the results when the truth came out.

When these people come to you and enjoy themselves telling you Charles Ramirez said *this* or Charles Ramirez thinks *that,* let it be known now that it's a lie. If you did not hear it from Charles Ramirez himself chances are it is a lie, and these people need to get a life for themselves!

Explain Yourself Not Liking Charles Ramirez For 30 Years And Not Consider It As Hate

Explain not liking someone for so long that person considers it as hate. You can explain yourself that you don't hate the person, but if you don't take the initiative to prove it, that person has that right to say you hate him. Take the initiative and prove to that person.

If you're one of those people who doesn't like Charles Ramirez, ask yourself how long are you going to not like him. There are those who don't like Charles for over 30 years! Charles is 44 as of this writing. To not like someone for *this* long you can't say this isn't considered as hate.

Understand that those who don't like Charles are not taking the initiative to do anything with Charles about it! They're living a success not liking Charles Ramirez; otherwise, why aren't they taking the initiative to do anything with Charles about it? And you wonder why Charles is the way he is…?

Imagine having so many people not liking you they instigate others into not liking you either. Imagine coming into a room and no one acknowledges you and keeps their distance from you. Imagine you taking the initiative talking to them and they show you hate and walk away.

Describe yourself when you see Charles entering the room. Do you not like him so much you don't acknowledge him entering the room? Do you keep your distance from him? Do you enjoy yourself instigating others into not liking him they start to humiliate him for no reason at all?

No one ever said they hated Charles Ramirez, yet they *show* it through negligence and never wanting to see him again. They're *not interested.* Describe the success these people need to be motivated into not liking Charles for so long. Describe the success they got from not liking Charles for so long.

Describe the difficulty you have liking Charles. Describe the successes Charles made to make it difficult for you to like him. Describe the actions Charles did to make it difficult for you to like him. Describe the choice you made to make it difficult for you to like Charles.

Listen to the silence when Charles Ramirez enters the room. Do you really this is respect being shown to Charles? Look at their faces. They don't like Charles so much that if some people enjoy themselves hurting Charles these people feel that Charles *deserves* it. They turn their heads.

If you've been not liking Charles Ramirez for over thirty years, how can you say it's not hatred? You can get people to say that you don't hate Charles, but if you don't take the initiative to prove that, well those 30 or so years can be considered as hatred!

You can't just come out of nowhere and say you don't hate Charles just like *that* after not liking him for over thirty years. If Charles hasn't seen you in a long time and he *knows* you don't like him, how can he not take it as you hating him?

Hatred is a strong word. Hatred also comes in many forms. If Charles knows so many people don't like him for so long, and he doesn't hear from them or see them anymore, how can he not take it as them hating him? Imagine the burden it is for Charles to carry.

You may have a lot of people not liking you for so long and you can go on to say a lot of people hate you too. You may enjoy yourself getting all the hatred from those people who don't like you. Describe yourself handling the hatred. Is it really easy...?

Describe the people in Charles's life who don't like him for so long. Do you know who they are? Are you going to judge Charles by how long they didn't like him or even hated him? Are you going to follow up on what they do and not like him or hate him just the same?

Describe the people *not* in Charles's life who don't like him for so long. How can you not consider this as hate? 30 years is a long time. Describe the success they achieved for hating Charles for so long. Describe their reactions. Are they enjoying themselves reading about this?

Describe the ongoing price Charles has to pay living this burden of so many people not liking him so long they're living a success hating him. Describe the silent treatment Charles has to face every day of his life because so many people hate him. Describe the ongoing price...

Subject To A Higher Review

Imagine God watching you enjoy yourself teasing, embarrassing, and humiliating Charles Ramirez to a point where you accuse him of crimes, and he gets brutally and wrongfully punished. Imagine God changing the rules for Charles because of the teasings, the embarrassments, the humiliations, and the punishments you enjoy yourself with.

God is watching you enjoy yourself do wrong against Charles. God has watched you do wrong against Charles and enjoy yourself in the success – living so far away from Charles, acting like Charles doesn't exist when you see him face-to-face, avoiding him, pulling him to the side and punish him.

Understand that God knows no matter how many mistakes Charles Ramirez made in his life. God knows Charles is a good person. For you to enjoy yourself teasing, embarrassing, and humiliating Charles to a point of physical punishment shows the *true* persona of defying God you do through Charles.

Imagine the things God has for you. Just because you think Charles Ramirez is a good person that he prays for you, or you *think* Charles prays for you, doesn't mean God has something for you in penance. You enjoyed yourself seeing Charles physically hurt, just to see what Charles can or can't do.

Describe the benefits you got teasing, embarrassing, humiliating, and punishing Charles. Describe the benefits God has for Charles taking all your teasings, embarrassments, humiliations, and punishments. Describe the things God has for you teasing Charles, embarrassing Charles, humiliating Charles, and punishing Charles. Is it all good…?

You can go to church, confess, and make yourself a better person all you want to, but if you're keeping the benefits and successes you made teasing Charles, embarrassing Charles, humiliating Charles, and punishing Charles, you may be making it harder for yourself than it has to be, wouldn't you?

God is watching you *all the time!* You can lock your doors, lock your windows, close the drapes, close the blinds, turn off the big lights and leave that small desk lamp on showing that one success you have from embarrassing and humiliating Charles. *God is still watching you and hearing you.*

God is watching Charles too. He's watching Charles feel the pain from the teasings, the embarrassments, the humiliations, and the physical and mental punishments you enjoyed yourself putting him through! He watches Charles remembering it all! He's allowing Charles to *write* about it just much as you revel in it!

If you're going to own up and say God is watching you just to enjoy yourself embarrassing and humiliating Charles some more, you're owning up for all the wrong reasons. Just because you think Charles has to go through it all the punishments to be good doesn't mean it's right all the time.

There's always a guarantee that God is watching you enjoy yourself coming up with embarrassing and humiliating ideas to tease Charles Ramirez with, just as He has a guarantee for you to *answer* tothese embarrassments, humiliations, teasings, and punishments. It's not for Charles to embarrass you back!

With all the teasings, the embarrassments, the humiliations, and the punishments you enjoyed yourself putting Charles Ramirez through, not to mention the rejections most ladies put on him, how do you know God isn't changing the rules for Charles, tapping him on the shoulder saying to him you can be…?

All the teasings, the embarrassments, the humiliations, and the punishments explain the problems you have with Charles Ramirez being better than you and, God willing, *sexier* than you to the ladies! And to the "ladies" who manipulated you into teasing Charles are no better! God watched those ladies try to emasculate Charles.

Describe the setbacks in your life, especially those that may be connected to you enjoying yourself teasing, embarrassing, humiliating, and punishing Charles. If, as you say, those setbacks made you stronger, describe that strength. If that strength isn't humility, you're not as strong as you think you are…

God is watching you enjoy yourself teasing, embarrassing, humiliating, and punishing Charles when Charles didn't do *anything* to you. Through that, God may have change the rules for people like Charles Ramirez just for the excessive punishments you enjoy yourself dishing out to Charles and people like him.

The Face Of Asian-America

Recognize there is a face of Asian-America. There are so many qualities that make every Asian-American worthy of being the face of Asian-America. Fortunate few show it in their own way. Then there are those who enjoy themselves exploiting the flaws and say this is the face of Asian-America.

If you're one of those who think Charles Ramirez is not the face of Asian- America, if you're one of those who take or have taken one look at him and quick to think or say he is not the face of Asian-America, you don't know what Charles went through in his life.

Understand that just because you don't know who Charles Ramirez is, just because Charles isn't you and that he "doesn't know" what you went through in life, doesn't mean Charles can't be the face of Asian-America. Charles was born in South Philadelphia, raised in Willingboro, NJ, and is now living back in Philly.

Imagine the face of Asian-America based on individual qualities rather than cultural standards. Imagine the face of Asian-America recognized by people of *all* races in this country. Imagine the face of Asian-America with a name everyone can recognize (*Charles Ramirez*). Imagine the face of Asian- America born here in the United States!

I'M NOT A BLACK SLAVE DESCENDANT!

Describe the face of Asian-America based on the Asian-American you know of. Describe the face of Asian-America living across the street, around the block, down the street or *right next door* to you. Describe the face of Asian- America at your job. Describe the face of Asian-America living outside the city limits.

Charles Ramirez is the face of Asian-America! Just because he doesn't have People Magazine or any other magazine featuring him repeatedly in pictures doesn't make him any less the face of Asian-America, even though he would *like* that opportunity as often as it comes. Believe that he can be the face of Asian-America.

Prepare for the many faces of Asian-America! There are generations and generations of Asian-Americans *born and raised* in the United States of America, just like Charles Ramirez. Prepare for the recognition, the achievements, and the success these faces of Asian-America will accomplish. Prepare for a *new* beginning…the face of Asian-America!

Notice the younger generation now. These are the future faces of Asian- America. As much as they learn their culture, they're learning what goes on around them here in their own homes. They do things to contribute to the community. They volunteer. They just don't let their Asian culture define them.

Allow yourself to know the face of Asian-America. Allow yourself to know the name of the face of Asian-America. Don't deny yourself the opportunity of knowing the face of Asian-America. There is no more time to compromise yourself nor the face of Asian-America. Allow yourself learning the face of Asian-America.

Enjoy the face of Asian-America. If you enjoy the face of an African- American, the face of a Caucasian-American, or even the face of a Native- American, you can enjoy the face of an Asian-American! Enjoy living next door to the face of Asian-America. Enjoy working at the same job with the face of Asian-America.

Break Your Silence!

Charles Ramirez would like to talk to people, but he's sick and tired of the tolerance and the indifference. Charles is sick and tired of having to talk to someone first in order for that someone to talk to Charles at all! Charles isn't the one not interested in talking to Charles!

Those of you ladies who show Charles so much tolerance and so much indifference, then turn around and show additional emotional reaction to other guys who aren't even your husbands or boyfriends...this includes you, too! Break the silent treatment towards Charles. He can only take so much silence from you.

This is the real reason why Charles doesn't talk to people altogether. Charles faced and heard more than his fair share of so many people's imposing, confronting, or violent voice tones. They take more initiative in talking to Charles than most of you do ina lifetime. Break your silence!

Describe the times when you took all the people's imposing and violent attitude vocal tone to a point where you had to feel humbled beyond belief. Describe the times when you felt that you lost that trust. Describe the silence you got after all the violent vocal tones. Think back...

Describe your thoughts and feelings you would like to talk with Charles. Do any of you know what to talk about and feel for once you see Charles? Will your pre-conceived ideas hurt, embarrass, and humiliate Charles, or will your ideas heal, uplift and encourage positively and emotionally? Describe...

You ask yourself why does Charles allow so much imposing and violent attitude vocal tones from so many people? Ask yourselves why are they the only people taking the initiative talking to Charles first! Ask yourselves why are they the only people INTERESTED in talking to Charles! Ask yourselves, ladies!

Now is not the time to hurt, to embarrass, and to humiliate Charles some more with your imposing, confronting and violent voice tones and words! Break your silence, just don't be violent! Heal, uplift, and encourage. Just because Charles seems to be doing well doesn't mean he's not going around embarrassed.

Hear them talking about Charles "whining and complaining" after reading this? If they talk about themselves like this, would they describe themselves as "whining and complaining"? NO! They'd make themselves some sort of popular standard that you should follow along! Another reason why Charles himself doesn't talk much to anyone...

This isn't to say ladies have to talk to Charles the second you see him or when he makes his appearance. You talk about popularity and attention...how much more popular does Charles have to be for not being INTERESTED enough? What will it take to get the ladies' attention?

Don't Explain Yourself...

Don't explain yourself to Charles saying that you'd treat the same way the Black Slave Mentality treated Charles at the job! Don't explain yourself to Charles saying that you'd humiliate him to do the job just as much as the Black Slave Mentality did! You're not a Black Slave Mentality!

You act like Charles doesn't measure up to you. You set yourself at a popular or higher standard than Charles, and what better way to show that than having Charles face the Black Slave Mentality every day at the job? You think you're better than both Charles and the Black Slave Mentality?

There's the Black Slave Mentality. There's the black manager. There's the black business. What makes you think the Black Slave Mentality didn't elevate themselves up the corporate ladder? You're working 40+ hours a week with no rest! The Black Slave Mentality has no problem with you working those hours!

What does it say about you explaining that you'd humiliate Charles the same way the Black Slave Mentality did on the job? What do you have to gain from it? Popularity? Attention from the ladies? Instigating trouble between Charles and the Black Slave Mentality just so you can slip away and do what you want?

You're comfortable with your job position. You don't want anything to do with either Charles nor the Black Slave Mentality, but when the Black Slave Mentality riles Charles up to get your attention, you're quick to side with the Black Slave Mentality! This is how you resolve issues?

Charles Ramirez isn't the Black Slave Mentality! That's the comedy and the drama material the actual Black Slave Mentality needs to confuse and distract. Charles isn't coming up with all this material all by himself to write about! The Black Slave Mentality makes an example of himself through Charles.

You have better things to do than explaining to Charles saying that you'd humiliate him on the job the same way the Black Slave Mentality humiliated Charles. Remember the times the Black Slave Mentality humiliated you to do your job. how did you feel from facing their humiliating?

Hear the silence and the negligence Charles gets now! How many of you wish you humiliated Charles to do the jobs you don't want to do? How many of you have humiliated Charles to do things for your enjoyment? How many of you think that Charles is living easier than you?

Don't explain yourself to Charles saying that you'd humiliate him to do the job just as much as the Black Slave Mentality did! You have better things to do than explaining that! Charles Ramirez has been humiliated more times than he cares to remember! And don't act like he doesn't exist either!